CENGAGE Learning

Drama for Students, Volume 7

Staff

Editorial: David M. Galens, *Editor.* Tim Akers, Andrea Henry, Mark Milne, and Kathleen Wilson, *Contributing Editors.* James Draper, *Managing Editor.* David Galens and Lynn Koch, *"For Students" Line Coordinators.* Jeffery Chapman, *Programmer/Analyst.*

Research: Victoria B. Cariappa, *Research Manager.* Andrew Guy Malonis, Barbara McNeil, Gary J. Oudersluys, Maureen Richards, and Cheryl L. Warnock, *Research Specialists.* Patricia Tsune Ballard, Wendy K. Festerling, Tamara C. Nott, Tracie A. Richardson, Corrine A. Stocker, and, Robert Whaley, *Research Associates.* Phyllis J. Blackman, Tim Lehnerer, and Patricia L. Love, *Research Assistants.*

Permissions: Maria Franklin, *Permissions Manager.* Kimberly F. Smilay, *Permissions*

Specialist. Kelly A. Quin, *Permissions Associate.* Sandra K. Gore, *Permissions Assistant.*

Graphic Services: Randy Bassett, *Image Database Supervisor.* Robert Duncan and Michael Logusz, *Imaging Specialists.* Pamela A. Reed, *Imaging Coordinator.* Gary Leach, *Macintosh Artist.*

Product Design: Cynthia Baldwin, *Product Design Manager.* Cover Design: Michelle DiMercurio, *Art Director.* Page Design: Pamela A. E. Galbreath, *Senior Art Director.*

and other applicable laws. The authors and editors of this work have added value to the underlying factual material herein through one or more of the following: unique and original selection, coordination, expression, arrangement, and classification of information. All rights to this publication will be vigorously defended.

This book is printed on acid-free paper that meets the minimum requirements of American National Standard for Information Sciences—Permanence Paper for Printed Library Materials, ANSI Z39.48-1984.

ISBN 0-7876-4081-6
ISSN 1094-9232
Printed in the United States of America

10 9 8 7 6 5 4

Peter Pan

Sir J(Ames) M. Barrie 1904

Introduction

Peter Pan, which was alternately titled "The Boy Who Would Not Grow Up," was first performed in London, England, on December 27, 1904, at the Duke of York Theatre. It has since become one of the most widely performed and adapted children's stories in the world. It is also Barrie's best-known work, though he was a prolific author writing in a number of genres. Critics believe that one reason *Peter Pan* was successful from the first is that Barrie combined fantasy and adventure in a way not done before. The play offers a fresh means of storytelling that appeals to both adults and children. While children enjoy the imaginative story and flights of fancy, adults can relate to Peter Pan's desire to forego mature responsibilities and live in the moment. Roger Lancelyn Green wrote in his book *Fifty Years of Peter Pan:* "*Peter Pan* is the only children's play that is also a great work of literature."

The text of the play has evolved since it was first performed in 1904. The original stage production of *Peter Pan* was only three acts. Barrie let the story grow through several novels and different versions of the stage play to arrive at a standardized text by 1928. The playwright claimed that he did not remember writing the play, which began as a backyard amusement for some of his young friends. After its London debut, *Peter Pan* became an annual Christmas event in that city's theater district for several decades. The play has also been adapted into a musical stage version as well as several different kinds of movies. Ironically, considering the play's prominent theme of motherhood, Peter Pan is traditionally played by a young woman, while Nana the dog is usually played by a man in a dog suit.

Author Biography

J. M. Barrie was born on May 9, 1860, in Kirriemuir, Scotland, a village located in the Lowlands. He was the son of a poor weaver, David, and his wife, Margaret Ogilvy Barrie. Barrie was the second youngest of ten children and one of only several to survive infancy. Barrie's mother ensured that he received an education, and the playwright eventually received his M.A. from Edinburgh University in 1882. After Barrie's elder brother and Margaret Barrie's favorite son died when Barrie was six, he took it upon himself to take his brother's place. The author's relationship with his mother was unusually close and was often based in a fantasy world due to Margaret's bedridden condition. Barrie's complex relationship with his mother is thought by many to be the inspiration for the mother-worship that critics feel is central to *Peter Pan.*

Barrie began his writing career as a journalist soon after graduation from Edinburgh, first in Nottingham, then back in Scotland, and finally, London. In the late-1880s, Barrie published several novels and short stories. His first bestseller was 1891's *The Little Minister.* In that same year Barrie began writing plays and playlets, beginning with a one-act burlesque entitled *Ibsen's Ghost, or, Toole up to Date.* After successfully turning *The Little Minister* into a play in 1897, Barrie focused almost exclusively on the theatre. From 1901 until 1920, he wrote one play per year. One of Barrie's most famous plays during this period was 1902's *The Admirable Crichton,* a combination of fantasy and social commentary. These same elements were employed in Barrie's best-known work—and his only play intended explicitly for a young audience —*Peter Pan,* first produced in 1904.

The play had its roots in a novel Barrie published in 1902, *Little White Bird,* written for some young friends of Barrie, the Davies. Barrie met the family in London's Kensington Gardens in 1897 and was immediately enamored with the three young boys, George, Jack, and Peter, as well as their mother, Sylvia. Barrie befriended the family, spending considerable time with them over the years (the head of the Davies household, Arthur Davies, did not always like the situation but tolerated it nonetheless). Barrie worshiped Sylvia much like he did his own mother. This relationship was developed to the exclusion of Barrie's wife, the actress Mary Ansell, whom he had married in 1894. They divorced in 1909, their marriage apparently unconsummated. In many ways, Barrie was like Peter Pan, a man who had not fully matured.

After *Peter Pan* and several novelizations of the story, Barrie continued writing notable plays. Most were adult dramas and comedies that frequently played with fantasy, including *Dear Brutus* (1917). Barrie's success as a playwright allowed him to be generous with funds, and he gave often to individuals as well as important causes. Barrie ceased to write plays until a year before his death when he suddenly produced two Biblical dramas. Barrie died on June 19, 1937, in London.

Plot Summary

Act I

Peter Pan opens in the nursery of the Darling family household in Bloomsbury, London. The family is somewhat impoverished, employing Nana, a Newfoundland dog, as the three children's nurse. When the play's action begins, Nana is putting the youngest Darling child, Michael to bed, while Mrs. Darling prepares to go out for dinner with her husband. Wendy and John, the eldest and middle, respectively, play at being their parents for her. While Nana sees to the children. Mrs. Darling confides to her husband that she saw the face of a little boy at the window trying to get in and that she has seen it before. She almost caught him once but only managed to snare his shadow, which she has kept rolled up in a drawer. Mrs. Darling also describes a ball of light accompanying him.

Mr. Darling declares that he is sick of Nana working in the nursery and takes her to be tied up in the yard. Wendy hears Nana's barking, noting that the sound is one of danger and warning, not unhappiness. Despite her reservations about leaving her brood, Mrs. Darling tucks the children in bed and departs, turning out their light as she goes. Right after she leaves, Tinkerbell and Peter Pan enter, looking for Peter's shadow. Peter finds the shadow but cannot reattach it. His efforts awaken

Wendy. She learns that he does not have a mother and that she must never touch him. She finally realizes that he cannot reattach his shadow, and she sews it back on for him. She tries to kiss him, but he is ignorant of this simple display of affection. Instead, he gives Wendy an acorn button which she puts around her neck. He tells her about fairies and the Lost Boys and introduces her to Tinkerbell.

Peter reveals that none of the Lost Boys have mothers, so he comes to the Darling children's window to hear their stories and relate them to his friends. Wendy says that she knows lots of stories, so Peter teaches her how to fly so she can come to Never Land and tell stories to the Lost Boys. She insists that her brothers learn to fly as well, though Peter is not as interested in teaching them. Peter blows fairy dust on them and the children fly away to Never Land. Mr. and Mrs. Darling come home to find their children's beds empty.

Act II

In Never Land, the Lost Boys wait for Peter to return. They discuss their fear of pirates and how they do not remember their mothers. The pirates approach, lead by Captain Hook, and the boys hide in the trees. Captain Hook orders his crew to look for the boys, especially their leader, Peter Pan, because he cut Hook's arm off and the Captain wants revenge. Hook decides to catch the boys by leaving poisoned cake out that will kill them. Tiger Lily and her band of Indians make a brief appearance, and they see the pirates. They decide that they will scalp them when they catch them.

Following the pirates' departure and Peter and the Darling children's arrival, the Lost Boys emerge from their hiding places. Tinkerbell tricks the boys into shooting an arrow at Wendy. Wendy falls to the ground and seems dead. Peter lands. Wendy is very much alive: the arrow hit the acorn button Peter gave her. Tinkerbell is unhappy to learn that Wendy is alive, and Peter sends her away.

Peter decides that they will build a house around the still-prostrate Wendy. While Peter and the Lost Boys gather material, Michael and John land. They cannot believe where they are, and Peter shortly employs them in the building of their house. Once the structure is built around her, Wendy wakes up. Everyone begs her to be their mother. After a moment of hesitation, she agrees and begins to tell them the story of Cinderella.

Act III

Peter and the boys play in the Mermaid's Lagoon, trying unsuccessfully to catch a mermaid to show Wendy. Peter tells Wendy about Marooners' Rock, where sailors are left to die by drowning in the tide. The boys sense danger, and they all hide underwater. Two of Hook's pirates show up with a captive Tiger Lily and her Indians. They leave their captives on the rock. Peter imitates Captain Hook's voice and tells the pirates to untie their prisoners. The pirates follow his orders and release Tiger Lily, but the real Captain Hook arrives.

Hook tells his pirates that the boys have found a mother and that all is lost. One of Hook's men suggests that they capture Wendy and all the boys, kill the boys, then make Wendy their mother. Hook learns of the voice, Peter's, that commanded them to free Tiger Lily and communicates with it. Peter tells Hook that he is Hook. The real Hook asks many questions, but cannot figure the situation out. Finally, Peter tells Hook who he is, and leads an attack on the pirates. All the boys, except Peter, manage to capture the pirates dinghy and float away. Wendy and Peter are left stuck on the rock. The tide starts to come in, and Wendy makes her escape by holding on to the tail of a kite. Peter stays behind, hiding in a floating bird's nest.

Act IV

All of the children manage to make it back to their underground home. Tiger Lily and her Indians guard the children from the pirates above ground. Wendy has done the laundry and is serving the boys, save Peter, a pretend meal, as is done in New Land. The boys bicker among themselves, and it is revealed that Wendy regards Peter as the father of the bunch.

Peter returns and greets the Indians, thanking them for guarding his home. While the boys get ready for bed, Peter is concerned that it is only "pretend" that he is the father. When Wendy questions him, he tells her that he feels like her son, not the father to her mother. The boys return and under Wendy's orders, climb into bed. The story she tells them is about her own home—her father, mother, and Nana—and her brothers immediately recognize it. Wendy ends the story by saying that she knows the mother is leaving the window open for the children, hoping they will return and fly through it. But when she implies that she and her brothers will eventually return, Peter is unhappy. Despite this, Wendy decides that they will return to their parents. She asks Peter to make the appropriate arrangements.

Tinkerbell is to guide the Darlings home, but she tries to refuse the task. The boys beg Wendy not to leave, but she quiets them by telling them to come back with her. Her parents, she is sure, will adopt the Lost Boys. Peter refuses to join them, though Wendy wants him to come along as well. As Tinkerbell leads them away, the Pirates attack the Indians, many of whom perish. Hook's crew takes Tiger Lily and several others prisoners. Hook has other pirates wait, and when Peter is deceived into believing the attack is over, everyone leaves. Captain Hook is right there and everyone, except Peter who is asleep, has been captured. Tinkerbell wakes Peter and tells him what has happened. Peter vows to rescue Wendy.

Act V, scene 1

On the pirate ship, Hook is happy, convinced that Peter is dead from the poison he left. Hook calls up the prisoners, telling them that six will walk the plank but two can become his cabin-boys. The boys refuse to work for him, and Wendy is brought up to witness their deaths.

Unbeknownst to Hook, Peter is swimming the waters around the ship, pretending to be a crocodile (the animal Hook most fears). Tinkerbell's light flits around, distracting the pirates, while Peter climbs aboard and hides in the cabin. Hook orders one of his men to fetch the cat, but the pirate does not return for he is killed in the cabin. Hook sends several other men inside, and they are all killed. This scares the pirates and they believe they are doomed. The boys are driven into the cabin, Peter releases their manacles, and they find hiding places from which to attack.

Hook decides to throw Wendy overboard to change their luck. Peter reveals himself then, and the boys attack. The battle finally comes down to Peter and Hook in a sword fight. When that reaches a stalemate, Hook arranges for the ship to be blown up in two minutes. Peter finds the bomb in time. Hook is finally defeated and eaten by a crocodile.

Act V, scene 2

In the Darling household nursery, Mrs. Darling waits for her children's return. Mr. Darling and Nana have switched places for his earlier actions which led to the loss of their children. Peter precedes the children and convinces Tinkerbell to bar the window to the nursery shut so the children will think they are unwanted. When he hears Mrs. Darling's sorrow, he opens the window again, and the children return. Michael and John are momentarily disoriented but decide to creep into bed. The family reunites, then brings the rest of the Lost Boys into the house.

Peter calls Wendy, and Mrs. Darling offers to adopt him, too, but he refuses. Mrs. Darling offers that Wendy can visit Peter once a year for spring cleaning.

Characters

Mr. George Darling

Mr. Darling is married to Mary Darling and is the father of the Darling children. A childish man, he is rather brusque to his children and Nana. Mr. Darling tries to trick Michael into taking his medicine by not taking his own. He also insists on tying up Nana outside which leads to Peter Pan taking the children to Never Land. Mr. Darling does pay the price in the end: he is forced to live in Nana's kennel while the children are missing. He is remorseful for his actions and is happy when they return.

John Darling

John is the middle Darling child. When *Peter Pan* opens, he does not like girls nor does he want to bathe. He plays house with his sister Wendy and only responds positively when she announces their child is a boy. When Peter comes, John is excited to learn to fly and go to Never Land to fight pirates. Still, he is the first to want to go home when Wendy tells her story about their parents. John has a sense of pride about his heritage. He refuses to be a pirate when he learns he would have denounce the British king.

Media Adaptations

- *Peter Pan* was adapted as a silent film in 1924. This version was released by Paramount and was directed by Herbert Brenon. It starred Betty Bronson as Peter Pan, Mary Brian as Wendy, and Virginia Brown Faire as Tinkerbell.

- An full-length animated version was filmed in 1953. Released by Disney, it was directed by Clyde Geronimi and Wilfred Jackson. It featured the voices of Bobby Driscoll as Peter Pan, Kathryn Beaumont as Wendy, and Hans Conreid as both Captain Hook and Mr. Darling.

- A live television version was performed on NBC in 1955, then done again live in 1956. Both versions featured Mary Martin as Peter Pan, Kathleen Nolan as Wendy, and Cyril Ritchard as Captain Hook.

- A made-for-television adaptation was shown on NBC in 1976. It featured Mia Farrow as Peter Pan and Danny Kaye as Captain Hook.

- An animated television series based on the stage play was shown in syndication in 1990. Known as *Peter Pan and the Pirates,* it featured the voice of Tim Curry as Captain Hook and Jason Mardsen as Peter Pan.

Mrs. Mary Darling

Mrs. Darling is the loving mother of the Darling children. Where her husband loses his temper, she is patient and kind with both George and the children. Mrs. Darling is the first to have noticed Peter Pan's face in the window and fears for her children's safety. She is devastated when her worst fears are confirmed and is ecstatic when they return.

Michael Darling

Michael is the youngest of the Darling children and the littlest when the arrive in Never Land. He is obstinate and does not want to go to bed or take his medicine. When Peter comes into their nursery, he is the first to fly. During the battle on the pirate ship, Michael kills a pirate. When they finally return home, Michael is slightly confused as to who his mother really is and he is also disappointed to find that his father is smaller than the pirate he killed.

Wendy Darling

Wendy Darling is a young girl for whom Peter Pan shows great affection. She is the eldest child of Mr. and Mrs. Darling. Wendy likes to play house, even before Peter convinces her to fly to Never Land. She is a fairly obedient and helpful child, mindful of her responsibilities. For example, Wendy helps her father get Michael to take his medicine and is quick to point out when her father tries to cheat. When Peter finds his shadow in a drawer and cannot reattach it, Wendy solves the problem and sews it back on for him. In Never Land, Wendy takes the role of the Lost Boys' mother very seriously, though she says she has no experience. She does her best to fulfill the role, but when she realizes how much her absence must hurt her own mother, she insists on returning home bringing along the Lost Boys so they can be adopted.

Wendy is also patient and kind. She tries to teach Peter about kissing but does not embarrass him when it is obvious he does not know what she is talking about. When Peter is uncomfortable about being the boys' father, Wendy accepts this, too. Wendy also has a whimsical side: she desperately wants to catch a mermaid.

First Twin

See The Lost Boys

Captain Jas Hook

Captain Hook is a pirate who lives in Never Land. He is the mortal enemy of Peter Pan because Peter severed his arm in a battle and fed it to a crocodile. Hook spends the play trying to enact revenge on Peter Pan and the Lost Boys. When one of his pirate band learns that Peter has Wendy, he captures her, hoping to make her the mother for the ship. Hook also succeeds in capturing the Darling brothers and the Lost Boys, but when Peter and Hook fight their final battle, Hook loses and is eaten by a crocodile.

Hunkering

See The Lost Boys

The Lost Boys

The six Lost Boys live in Never Land, and include Peter Pan among their number as their leader. They are boys who had fallen out of their carriages when their nurses were not looking. No one claimed them and after seven days, they were sent to Never Land. Since they have no mother, they are excited by Wendy's presence and do everything to please her. Following Peter's lead, they also defend her. When given the opportunity to go home and be adopted by the Darling family, they return to England.

Nana

Nana is dog employed as a nurse in the Darling household. She gives the children their medicine, puts them to bed, and tends to their needs much like a human nanny.

Nibs

See The Lost Boys

Peter Pan

Peter Pan is the ageless boy who is at the play's center. He ran away from home when he found out what kind of responsibilities he would have as an adult. He does not want to grow up at all. As the captain of the Lost Boys, however, he does lead them and tell them stories. He also takes it upon himself to find them a mother, which he does in bringing Wendy to Never Land. Despite his actions to the contrary, Peter professes his disdain for responsibility. When Wendy sets him up as the Boy's father, he does not want the position. He tells Wendy that he looks upon her as his mother also.

Peter's refusal to grow up also affects his memory. He cannot remember incidents for very long after they happen. He is also ignorant of basic human interactions such as kissing and tells Wendy he can never be touched. But Peter is not afraid to fight. When Tiger Lily is in jeopardy, he saves her. When Wendy and the Lost Boys are captured by Captain Hook, he battles and saves them. For the most part, however, Peter is content to play his pipes and make merriment.

Second Twin

See The Lost Boys

Slightly

See The Lost Boys

Tootles

See The Lost Boys

Tiger Lily

Tiger Lily is an Indian who leads a tribe of men in Never Land. She is a friend of Peter Pan's. When he rescues her from Captain Hook, she repays the favor by guarding his underground home.

Tinkerbell

Tinkerbell is a fairy who is the size of a fist. She got her name because she mends fairy pots and kettles. She appears as a ball of light who can dart quickly around rooms, and speaks only in bells. She is attached to Peter Pan, and follows him around everywhere. Tinkerbell is rather jealous of Wendy and tries to subvert the affection Peter Pan shows for her. She also risks her life for Peter, swallowing poison meant for him.

Themes

Sex Roles

Sex roles, especially motherhood, are explored in *Peter Pan*. Peter convinces Wendy to come to Never Land so she can see a mermaid, but he really wants her to act as a mother to himself and the Lost Boys. She is to tell them stories, like her own mother tells to her. Though Wendy admits she has no experience playing a mother role, she imitates her own mother's behavior and manages to win the boys over.

Peter is unwilling to play father to Wendy's mother, however. He will accept the role if it is just "pretend," but he is unwilling to accept actual responsibility. Though the exact role of "father" is not clearly defined in the play—Mr. Darling is more of a temperamental child than a nurturing, paternal figure—Peter is only willing to serve as the primary defender of the Lost Boys' home, little more. He is more concerned with adventure, having fun, and fighting pirates—aspects that conveniently fit into his role as a protector. Peter does not understand what being a father means. John tells the other Lost Boys at one point, "He did not even know how to be a father till I showed him." Peter tells Wendy, in roundabout fashion, that he only knows how to be a son, which frustrates other characters such as Tiger Lily.

Topics for Further Study

- Compare and contrast the standardized dramatic text of *Peter Pan* (1928) with any of the novelizations of the Peter Pan story that Barrie wrote. How do the demands of the different literary forms affect the basic plot?

- Research societal attitudes towards women and motherhood in turn-of-the-century England. How do these attitudes compare with the depictions of women in *Peter Pan?*

- The rights to *Peter Pan* have been owned by Disney for a number of years. Research how the character and the story have been modified, particularly in reference to Disney's immensely popular animated adaptation, since the debut of the stage play in 1904.

- Compare and contrast the character of Wendy Darling in *Peter Pan* with Alice in Lewis Carroll's children's fantasy book *Alice's Adventures in Wonderland.* How are their experiences in a fantastic land similar? Different? How does the fact that these characters are female affect their fantastic experiences?

Duty & Responsibility

Duty and responsibility—or a lack thereof—drive the actions of many characters in *Peter Pan.* Peter Pan wants to avoid all adult responsibility and goes to great lengths to achieve this goal. He refuses to play father to Wendy's mother, uncomfortable even when pretending the role. In the end, when Wendy and her brothers decide to go back home, Peter will not let himself be adopted by the Darlings as the other Lost Boys are. If he went back, he would eventually have to grow up, assume responsibility, and become a man. This is unacceptable to Peter so he stays alone in Never Land, and Wendy comes back annually to do his spring cleaning. Despite his fear of adulthood, Peter does his duty as captain of the Lost Boys and protector of Wendy (and Tiger Lily). He rescues all of them from Captain Hook's band of pirates. He can only be responsible in these types of situations.

Conversely, Wendy, Tiger Lily, and even Captain Hook exhibit a sense of responsibility. When each is in a leadership role—be it mother, Indian chief, or head pirate—they act as their duties require them. Even the Lost Boys fulfill their responsibilities as followers of Peter. But only Wendy has a duty-related dilemma. She realizes that she is a daughter. As eldest child and the one who led her brothers away to Never Land, Wendy comes to understand that her own parents might need their children. Wendy must fulfill her role as daughter and go back home because other people, besides the Lost Boys and Peter Pan, need her. She solves her dilemma by inviting everyone to come and live with the Darling family.

Good and Evil

In *Peter Pan,* the lines between good and evil seem clearly drawn on the surface. Peter, the Lost Boys, Wendy, and her brothers, as well as Tiger Lily and the Indians, are on the side of good. Captain Hook and his pirates are evil. They are pirates, an occupation that requires certain antisocial, criminal behaviors. Yet the distinction between good and evil is not as clearly defined as it initially appears. The Indians are after scalps when they encounter the pirates. Employing methods of questionable honor, Peter does lead Wendy and her brothers away from their home. Tinkerbell is jealous of Wendy and while she does heroically save Peter, she also tries on several occasions to cause Wendy considerable harm.

The antagonists of *Peter Pan* are more distinctly "bad," but they are also not as clearly developed as Peter, the Darling children, or the Lost Boys. In their limited time on stage, they are only shown scheming or fighting. Yet there is indication that they have more rounded characters. Like Peter and the Lost Boys, they also desire a mother, suggesting that much of their behavior might be tempered by a female influence. Yet because Barrie took more time in developing his protagonists, their motivations, while still essentially good, are more complex than Hook and the Pirates'.

Style

Setting

Peter Pan is a children's fantasy/adventure set in turn-of- the-century London and an imaginary place called Never Land. The action that takes place in London is focused in the nursery of the Darling household, located in the borough of Bloomsbury. Never Land is an island, and the action in these scenes takes place in the forest, including shelters both above and below ground; there is also a lagoon where mermaids swim. The other Never Land location is Captain Hook's pirate ship, the Jolly Roger, where the play's climactic battle takes place. These diverse settings emphasize the difference between reality and fantasy. Though the Darling household has a dog for a nanny (a slightly fantastic notion), the household is predominantly rooted in sober reality; order prevails within the home. In Never Land, there is no mature authority so the island features forest, lagoons, and pirate ships— things that appeal to a child's sense of adventure and fun. There is very little order or responsibility; the Lost Boys and the pirates are dutiful followers of their respective leaders, but there is little organization beyond obedience on the field of battle.

Special Effects

Peter Pan features numerous special effects to emphasize the fantastic elements, especially of the otherworldly Tinkerbell and Peter. Tinkerbell is a fairy. In the earliest productions, she was not played by a person but was merely a lighting effect (some latter-day productions have employed an actor to portray Tinkerbell, mostly informed by Walt Disney's animated adaptation of the play which depicted the fairy as an actual, tiny person). Tinkerbell often appeared as a ball of light created by light hitting an angled mirror, her voice a splash of bells. As little more than light and sound effects, Tinkerbell could appear otherworldly to the audience, able to flit about the stage very quickly. Like the fairy, Peter exhibits extra-human characteristics: he is able to fly, he is ageless, and much about his person defies reason—such as his shadow being detached from his body.

The special effects are an essential part of Barrie's play and a primary reason for its popularity among generations of audiences. For a production to be effective, the play must realistically present such things as Peter flying, a dog that acts human, and a magical fairy. Most productions of *Peter Pan* employ some type of wire and pulley system that enables stagehands to lift the actors off the ground and move them about as if they are flying. Nana the dog-nanny is frequently played by a human in costume. Various lighting and sound effects are used to convey Tinkerbell's presence and fairy-like abilities. If properly executed, these effects heighten the sense of fantasy and fun in the play.

Foreshadowing: Mother's Instinct

When the dramatic technique of foreshadowing is used in Barrie's play, it is most often in conjunction with mothers and mothering; maternal insights usually telegraph important events in the play. Mrs. Darling had previously seen Peter in the window when tucking her children into bed and reading them stories. She is reluctant to go out to dinner with her husband in Act I because of what she has seen. Her worst fears are realized when Peter does come back for his shadow and convinces the children to come to Never Land. When Wendy assumes the role of mother to the Lost Boys and her own little brothers, she, too, develops a mature instinct. While telling her "children" a story about her home, she realizes, with the help of John, that her mother probably misses her and that they must return home.

Historical Context

At the turn of the twentieth century, Great Britain was a formidable world power, controlling territory on nearly every continent. Queen Victoria ruled the country from 1837 until her death in 1901, and her influence on Great Britain was still felt in 1904 though her son Edward VII was on the throne. The Edwardian era was extravagant for those with money, but the difference between the rich and the poor was a sharply divided line. Though the United States was still a developing nation, its industrial power gave it a burgeoning reputation.

While London was the center of several international markets, including currency and commodities, there was economic doubt and tension after years of prosperity due to the Industrial Revolution of the late-nineteenth century. Certain commodities suffered while others prospered. Farmers who grew grains did not do as well as dairy or fruit farmers. Industry moved towards consolidations and concentrations of power, but exports continued to fall. Still, London was the capital of finance and banking, and this market made up for the overall trade deficits in other areas. The national average income continued to increase, but the gap between classes continued to grow.

Despite wage increases, there was a movement among laborers in Great Britain to organize. Both skilled and unskilled workers joined unions in record numbers to address their concerns. Many labor leaders professed socialist and Marxist beliefs. A political party often sympathetic to many of the concerns of workers and lower classes was the Liberal party. When they won parliamentary control in 1906, they addressed many social reform concerns. They made free meals available to poor schoolchildren and founded a medical service to address those children's health concerns. Still, poverty was widespread in England, with one study showing that 27% of the population of York lived below the poverty line.

One source of controversy in both Great Britain and the United States was the use of child labor in factories and mills. In the United States there was a call for regulations on the number of hours a child could work as well as a call for mandatory attendance at school. In 1904, the National Child Labor Committee was formed in the United States. The first child labor law was passed in the United States in 1908.

Women also worked in these factories and rarely received the same wages as men; women's job opportunities were limited to certain sectors as society still believed a woman's place was in the home. Some women in the United States demanded the right to vote to address these and other concerns while others organized their own unions and formed other groups to promote their agendas, which often focused on social welfare. The Women's Trade Union League (WTUL) was formed in the United States in 1903. A similar voting and social reform-minded organization was formed that same year in Britain. Called the Women's Social and Political Union, its leadership called for violent acts against unsympathetic forces and hunger strikes among its members to dramatize its message.

Compare & Contrast

- **1904:** Child labor is common in both the United States and Great Britain but is a source of controversy. Legislation is proposed to regulate it, including laws that would require children to spend a certain amount of time in school.
  Today: Child labor in American and England is highly restricted. Still, several American companies, including Nike, employ factories in developing countries to manufacture their goods at an extremely low cost. These factories often use child labor in sweatshop-like conditions.

- **1904:** People flying in airplanes is an almost unheard-of concept. The Wright brothers made their first successful flight in 1903.
  Today: Commercial air travel is common all over the world. Thousands of flights span the globe daily.

- **1904:** Women comprise nearly one-third of the workforce in the United States. They are confined to certain jobs, mostly of a domestic nature, and receive low pay.

Today: Women comprise approximately half the workforce in the United States. While job opportunities are available in nearly every field, on average women make less than 80% of their male counterparts.

- **1904:** Education has only recently been made compulsory in the United States and is still not required in Great Britain.

  Today: Education, at least to age 16, is mandated by law in the United States and Great Britain.

Critical Overview

When *Peter Pan* was first produced in London in 1904, it was an immediate success. Though it broke box-office records, its producers were unsure if the play would be successful at all because it was so unlike anything that had been staged before. Barrie was regarded as a genius in his day, not just for the childlike insights that inform *Peter Pan* but also for a number of the other plays the prolific author wrote. Max Beerbohm, writing in the *Saturday Review,* said: 'I know not anyone who remains, like Mr. Barrie, a child. It is this unparalleled achievement that informs so much of Mr. Barrie's later work, making it unique. This, too, surely is what makes Mr. Barrie the most fashionable playwright of his time. Undoubtedly, *Peter Pan* is the best thing he has done—the thing most directly from within himself. Here, at last, we see his talent in its full maturity."

Contemporary critics noted that the play has appeal for both children and adults. A reviewer from the *Illustrated London News* wrote: "There has always been much in Mr. Barrie's work, of the child for whom romance is the true reality and that which children of a larger growth called knowledge. Insofar as the play deals with real life, we think it a bit cruel."

Many critics praised Barrie for not condescending to children, for dealing frankly with the cruelties of real life. In his book *The Road to Never Land: A Reassessment of J. M. Barrie's Dramatic Art*, R. D. S. Jack argued, *"Peter Pan*, by highlighting the cruelty of children, the power-worship of adults, the impossibility of eternal youth, the inadequacy of narcissistic and bisexual solutions, presents a very harsh view of the world made palatable by humour and held at an emotional distance by wit and the dream." Jack concluded, *"Peter Pan* addresses children but it treats childhood neither sentimentally nor as a condition divorced from adulthood."

Other critics have found that some aspects of *Peter Pan* are overly sentimental, especially those scenes taking place in the Darling household. Defensive of such accusations, Roger Lancelyn Green, in his *Fifty Years of Peter Pan,* wrote: "Sometimes, be it admitted, he [Barrie] approached perilously near the borderlands of sentimentality: such moments are seized upon with uncritical zeal as examples of typical Barrie, and the whole condemned for the occasional blemish."

Peter Pan has also been examined by critics more closely from other angles. In *The Road to Never Land,* Jack explored *Peter Pan* in terms of a Barrie-created mythology. He wrote: "Barrie was intent on devising a structure which combined the demands of an artificial, perspectivist creation-myth with those of a drama addressing both adults and children."

Others have used psychological approaches to understand *Peter Pan* and what the play says about its author. Many critics believed that Barrie himself did not want to grow up and that the play is an extension of his own experiences. Green wrote in *J. M. Barrie: A Walck Monograph,* that "all of Barrie's life led up to the creation of Peter Pan, and everything that he had written so far contained hints or foreshadowings of what was to come." Critics have explored Barrie's complex relationship with the Davies family and his own mother, seeking to understand his motivations in the creation of *Peter Pan.*

Several critics have focused specifically on the themes of motherhood that pervade the play, arguing that Barrie idealizes mothers to a fault while fathers are portrayed as unloving. John D. Shout in *Modern Drama,* believed that Barrie used *Peter Pan* to further an agenda. He wrote, "*Peter Pan* may have come to life as a bunch of tales to beguile Barrie's young friends the Davies boys, but it ended up much more a sequence of object lessons for young women, and a far more artful set of lessons than the old manuals since the women are paying attention and can hardly suspect that they're being preached to." In the same essay, Shout added, "adult males in this play are simply cowards or cads which only serves further to elevate the women." This dichotomy continues to be a source of critical debate regarding *Peter Pan.*

What Do I Read Next?

- *Mary Rose* is a play written by Barrie in 1920. It concerns a woman who has returned home after living among fairies.

- *Charlotte's Web,* written by E. B. White in 1952, is a children's novel that also deals with motherhood (in this case a spider who nurtures a young pig) as well as the perils of maturity.

- *The Little White Bird; Or, Adventures in Kensington Gardens,* a novel written by Barrie in 1902, is a precursor to the story *of Peter Pan.*

- *Androcles and the Lion,* a 1913 play by George Bernard Shaw, is a children's farce that was written as a direct response to *Peter Pan.*

- *The Peter Pan Syndrome: Men Who Have Never Grown Up* (1983) is a nonfiction book by Dan Kileya. It is a psychological analysis of males in the United States.

Sources

Barrie, James. *Peter Pan, Or, the Boy Who Would Not Grow Up,* Scribner, 1928.

Beerbohm, Max. "The Child Barrie" in the *Saturday Review,* January 7, 1905, pp. 13–14.

Green, Roger Lancelyn. *Fifty Years of Peter Pan,* Peter Davies, 1954, pp. 2, 155.

Green, Roger Lancelyn. *J. M. Barrie: A Walck Monograph,* Henry Z. Walck, 1960, p. 34.

Jack, R. D. S. *The Road to the Never Land: A Reassessment of J. M. Barrie's Dramatic Art,* Aberdeen University Press, pp. 167–68, 170.

Review of *Peter Pan* in *The Illustrated London News,* January 7, 1905.

Shout, John D. "From Nora Helmer to Wendy Darling: If You Believe in Heroines, Clap Your Hands" in *Modern Drama,* 1992, p. 360.

Further Reading

Barrie, James. *Margaret Ogilvy,* Scribner, 1896.

> This is a biography Barrie wrote about his mother. It offers considerable insight into the playwright's psyche as well as the roots of his fascination with motherhood.

Birkin, Andrew. *J. M. Barrie and the Lost Boys: The Love Story That Gave Birth to Peter Pan,* Clarkson N. Potter, 1979.

> This book details the complex relationship between Barrie and the Davies family. It features pictures, letters, and other primary source information.

Jack, R. D. S. "The Manuscript of *Peter Pan*" in *Children's Literature,* 1990.

> This article discuses the original manuscript of *Peter Pan* and the evolution of the basic story.

Walbrook, H. M. *J. M. Barrie and the Theatre,* F. V. White & Co., 1922.

> This book offers both analyses of Barrie's plays, including *Peter Pan,* and background information on Barrie and his work.